MW00612461

Brand Names That Sell.

Brand Names That Sell.

by J. David Placek

Founder, Lexicon Branding

LEXICON®

Contents

Today, there is nothing easy about creating a brand name that sells. It takes more than creativity and marketing acumen. It takes clear thinking and unflinching resolve to invent something new and useful.

This small book was written to pass on to readers some of the insights we have gained by working on some of the most challenging assignments with some of the most talented clients across the globe.

Over the years, we have sought to apply a coherent set of ideas in remarkably different ways. One of the great joys of brand development is that each engagement is like starting over again.

—David Placek

Founder, Lexicon Branding

*"The difference between
the almost right word and the
right word is really a large
matter—it's the difference
between the lightning bug and
the lightning."*

—Mark Twain

1:

Options

Facts About Intel's Pentium®

Trailblazing computer chip that transformed Intel's business and became a billion-dollar brand. Once featured on the cover of *Fortune* as the leading player in "The New Computer Revolution."

CHANGE THE GAME.

The only way to truly change the game is to do something that no one else has done before.

Under Andy Grove's leadership, Intel moved an entire marketplace with one seven-letter word.

Pentium® is a registered trademark of Intel Corporation, and the brand name was created by Lexicon Branding, Inc.

Fact About Swiffer®

Procter & Gamble's second largest product, with $500 million in sales annually.

Make Every Letter Count.

Don't spend all of your creative energies on meaning. Sound and letter structure are equally important, especially in the global marketplace.

In 1999, when we presented Swiffer to P&G's President, Durk Jager, he quickly saw the idea of "swiftly and effortlessly sweeping and swiping."

Swiffer® is a registered trademark of Procter&Gamble Company, and the brand name was created by Lexicon Branding, Inc.

Facts About Apple's PowerBook® Computer

Apple's groundbreaking notebook with sales over $1 billion in its first year alone. In 2001, it was given the Design Excellence Awards' "Gold" status.

MAKE A PROMISE.

If you can make a promise and deliver on it, do it. It will make a lasting impression.

Two common words welded together created a powerful marketing tool for Apple. The first series of PowerBooks was hugely successful, capturing 40% of all laptop sales.

Fact About P&G's Febreze®

In 2012, it became one of Procter & Gamble's bona fide billion-dollar brands.

BE RELEVANT, BUT UNEXPECTED.

Starting with a very descriptive idea, like "fresh breeze," can lead you to an unexpected and distinctive new idea.

Febreze is one of P&G's most successful new product launches.

Fact About Tangerine®

ING DIRECT, Canada's largest online bank, became Tangerine in early 2014.

Be Counter-Intuitive.

It is one of the most effective options in your creative toolbox. Nothing generates more interest, and nothing communicates confidence better.

Changing Canada's largest online bank, ING DIRECT, to Tangerine does not fit the traditional model for naming a bank. However, we found ING DIRECT to be the opposite of traditional. The brightness and freshness of Tangerine was selected as "the perfect fit."

FACT ABOUT COLGATE'S WISP®

The world's first disposable toothbrush with a breath-freshening bead.

"Short Words Are the Best"

— Winston Churchill

With millions of trademarks around the world, it is almost impossible to uncover or create a three or four-letter word that's available, but in Lexicon's experience it is always worth the effort.

Wisp was the perfect fit for the world's lightest and smallest toothbrush.

BlackBerry®

Fact About BlackBerry®

By 2010, 80 million users worldwide.

Be Unpredictable.

It takes a lot to get attention these days. Surprising someone almost always works, especially if you can make a relevant connection. In the case of BlackBerry, you have a more natural and engaging way to communicate.

Fact About General Motors' OnStar®

6 million customers, $1.5 billion in annual sales.

Create a Visual Experience.

Nothing is more memorable than a tangible image, and from the beginning of time nothing is more recognized around the world than a star.

OnStar® is a registered trademark of General Motors Company, and the brand name was created by Lexicon Branding, Inc.

Fact About Coca-Cola's Dasani®

More than 200 million cases sold around the globe every year.

Be Different From the Rest.

In the USA alone, there are over 800 brands of bottled water. Most use place names like Poland Spring, or suggestive names like Aquafina. For The Coca-Cola Company to create a leader in the category, they had only one choice: invent something new.

Fact About Subaru's Outback®

Still one of the best-selling all-wheel drive cars in America.

Give Them Something to Think About.

Strategy is choosing to be different. In a world of Western auto brands, like Explorer or Pathfinder, Lexicon helped Subaru take a left turn towards Australia.

Outback® is a registered trademark of Subaru Inc., and the brand name was created by Lexicon Branding, Inc.

Explorer® is a registered trademark of Ford Motor Company.

Pathfinder® is a registered trademark of Nissan Motor Co. Ltd.

Fact About Upwave™

Upwave is a multi-platform entertainment brand focused on health, wellness and nutrition, launched by Turner Broadcasting System (TBS).

CAPTURE THE ACTION.

Whenever possible, bring motion and energy to the idea. The Kellogg Company did this in 1964 with the introduction of Pop-Tarts and never looked back. Two billion Pop-Tarts are sold every year.

"Upwave is excited to help people make positive choices in their lives through entertaining and engaging content," states Molly Battin, SVP and General Manager of Upwave. "Our goal is to inspire people to get up, get moving, and enjoy what it means to 'live life on the up'."

Fact About Gap's Piperlime®

Over $1 billion in total sales since its start in 2006.

Be Colorful.

Color never fails to bring energy and memorability. It is always worth exploring.

In the crowded and intensely competitive online marketplace, Piperlime stands out, fresh and bright.

Amplify.

Fact About Amplify®

Launched in 2013, Amplify is reimagining the way teachers teach and students learn. It is a significant step forward in building curriculum for the digital world.

"I Believe"

This is the foundation of every successful brand.

Amplify is a company and digital platform with the talent and energy to bring dramatic change to education in America's middle schools.

Our creative strategy was to find a real word that would communicate the promise that they were making to students, teachers and parents.

"We call it Amplify for a reason," states Chief Executive Joel Klein. "At every level of the educational enterprise we want to amplify, to empower teachers, to improve instruction, to get parents more involved."

Fact About Shield®

NVIDIA made a bold move by going beyond the processor business and creating their own device. According to Android Central, the Shield is the "Holy Grail of mobile devices for any gamer."

Form, Function & Behavior.

Form, function and behavior are creative avenues that should always be considered.

Sometimes the physical form of a product can be used to create a distinctive personality.

In this case, NVIDIA's bold move into gaming consoles, and the rather dramatic shield shape on the top of the console made it easy. According to The Verge, *the Shield is "a seriously impressive piece of hardware."*

Shield® is a registered trademark of NVIDIA Corporation, and the brand name was created by Lexicon Branding, Inc.

FACT ABOUT SCION®

The word *scion* comes from the old French word for "a shoot or twig."

Comfort and Popularity Don't Matter.

What matters is the ability of the word, real or invented, to weave a story that is larger than the brand itself.

In today's environment, it pays to be dangerous, provocative and confident. Let the other guys just fit in.

When Toyota engaged Lexicon the request was simple: to create a name that would attract young buyers, and help them build a very contemporary brand.

Fact About ooVoo®

In 2011, ooVoo launched its social video chat service on the iPhone platform making it a free video chat service across PC, Mac, iPhone and Android platforms.

Don't Underestimate Sound; It Matters.

By uniting meaning, sound and structure, the right name engages consumers on several levels and across the globe. Lexicon has invested millions of dollars of research in sound symbolism, the study of how specific sounds and letters make consumers feel.

In 2007, Arel, an Israeli company, engaged Lexicon to create a global brand for a video chat and messaging technology. Rather than focus on words, we directed our teams to create solutions focused entirely on sound.

2:

GUIDELINES

Rule No. 1

Don't Be Boring.

It is one of the most common mistakes. We are all far more interested in good stories rather than simple explanations. One of Albert Einstein's most popular quotes, "Imagination is more important than knowledge" applies equally well to brand names.

Rule No. 2

Be Suggestive, Never Descriptive.

In 1878, Procter & Gamble wanted its first brand—a new soap—to be named P&G White Soap.

William Procter insisted on a more distinctive name, then he ran across the word ivory *while reading a psalm. The rest is history.*

Rule No. 3

Don't Use Superlatives.

They only lead your customers to discount your story. The last thing they want is another overpromise.

Rule No. 4

Don't Be Frivolous.

In the words of
Claude Hopkins, the author
of Scientific Advertising*,*
"People don't buy from clowns."

Rule No. 5

You Don't Always Need a New Name.

Nomenclature can be used effectively to simulate interest and signal innovation.

Kindle Fire HDX

We used three simple letters to help Amazon launch its second generation Fire brand.

Rule No. 6

Think Again.

If you think your customers might have the same associations with words as you, think again.

Several years ago, we presented the name Java to a client who said, "Coffee makes me nervous," and rejected the name. A year later, Sun Microsystems launched Java, a language that later became a billion-dollar brand.

3:

STRATEGY

Why Can't We Just Extend Our Existing Brands?

If you want to grow, you need fresh ideas.

Where would these companies be without these new brands?

P&G & Swiffer

Levi's & Dockers

Toyota & Lexus

Apple & iPhone

Would P&G's Swiffer Be A Billion Dollar Brand If They Had Called It "Pro Mop"?

A new brand is a fundamental component of your next growth engine. Invest time and resources accordingly.

And never forget that your new name is the one thing your competitors cannot take away from you.

Keep
Positioning
Simple.

Who it's for, what it does,
and why people should buy it.
Period.

"Why we are here" makes
for a strong position and an
even better story.

A Brief for the Development of a Name Is *Different* Than a Brief for an Advertising Campaign.

(1) A naming brief makes sure that distinctiveness is a primary goal and that risk will be rewarded.

(2) A naming brief answers this fundamental question: How can the name help this new brand to become a winner?

(3) A naming brief defines a specific role for the name rather than the product itself, messaging or design.

(4) A naming brief tells the story of the brand so that the brand name becomes an essential part of the story—better yet, the title.

You Can't
Manage
a Creative
Process.
You Can Lead It.

Never write a brief for a creative team. Write it with them. Creative leadership is about encouragement, and the root word of encouragement is courage.

A truly creative meeting is one where you speculate, not evaluate. Talk to creative people about their ideas and their process; ask how they want a session to be run instead of setting the agenda. Encouragement generates creativity.

Peter Drucker once said that "it's not about being right along the way, it is about being effective in the end."

Ideas Need
to be
Nourished.

How many times do people actually say, "Tell me more about that idea"? That sets the tone for innovation. Start with the goal of understanding every idea presented and build from there. If you do that, you create a climate for innovation.

If you have been given the privilege of leading a branding program, focus on creating a climate for new ideas and innovation. Killing ideas is easy. Nurturing ideas is demanding.

Don't Let
a Committee
Select Your
Company's Next
Major Asset.

Clients often email a list of names to their teams and look for responses. This is a mistake. Naming decisions should never be made by committee. Breakthroughs do not lend themselves to consensus. Names need to be thought of in context, creatively, as tools to move a company's message forward. Do this yourself, then take the responsibility and risk to get it approved and launched.

What could be more rewarding?

About Lexicon

Since 1982, Lexicon Branding has created some of the world's most successful brand names, including BlackBerry, Intel's Pentium, Coca-Cola's Dasani, Toyota's Scion, General Motors' OnStar, Apple's PowerBook, P&G's Swiffer, and Subaru's Outback.

Lexicon is, arguably, the most inventive company in this category. In fact, over $350 billion of products have been sold that carry a brand name created by Lexicon.

Lexicon has also become a leader in corporate branding: Tangerine, a rebrand of ING DIRECT, is now Canada's largest online bank; Conversant, a rebrand of Mosaid, leads the field of intellectual property management; and in Texas, Aquacor has become the innovator in water purification systems.

LEXICON®

Yes to New Ideas.

978-0-692-20445-0

30 Liberty Ship Way, Suite 3360
Sausalito, CA 94965
415.332.1811
www.lexiconbranding.com